How to become a dinner party legend and avoid crippling psychological damage

Easy Dinner Party Recipes

Anvils are great conversation starters
at successful dinner parties,
providing no blacksmiths are present

LAGOON
BOOKS

NOT A FINE WAY TO
WELCOME YOUR GUESTS

Published in 2000 by
Lagoon Books
PO Box 311, KT2 5QW, UK
PO Box 990676, Boston, MA 02199, USA
WWW.LAGOONGAMES.COM

ISBN: 1902813162

First published in Australia in 1998 by
Pan Macmillan Australia Pty Limited

Copyright © 1998 Billy Blue Merchandising Pty Ltd

Recipes by Helen Tracey and Linda Kaplan

Additional writing by Ross Renwick

Supervising Chefs Matt Blundell and Gavin Cummins
of Kentra Double Bay Australia

Managing Director Aaron Kaplan Creative Director Ross Renwick

Printed in China

9	**STOCK**
9	**BROWN STOCK**
10	**VEGETABLE STOCK**
10	**WHITE STOCK**
10	**SAUCES**
11	**BASIC WHITE SAUCE**
11	**BECHAMEL SAUCE**
12	**DRESSINGS**
12	**VINAIGRETTE**
12	**MAYONNAISE**
13	**GREEN MAYONNAISE**
13	**AIOLI**
14	**HORS D'OEUVRES**
14	**STUFFED CHERRY TOMATOES**
15	**STEAK TARTARE**
16	**SOUPS**
16	**ZUCCHINI AND CORIANDER SOUP**
17	**TOMATO AND TARRAGON SOUP**
18	**CREAM OF JERUSALEM ARTICHOKE SOUP**
20	**FRENCH ONION SOUP**
21	**VICHYSSOISE**
22	**MUSHROOM VICHYSSOISE**
23	**CREAM OF WATERCRESS SOUP**
24	**SALADS**
24	**LEEK SALAD**
26	**GRAPEFRUIT AND GRAPE SALAD**
26	**WARM POTATO SALAD**
27	**GREEN BEANS WITH PINE NUTS**
28	**SPICY ORIENTAL BEEF SALAD**
29	**PRAWN, MUD CRAB AND MANGO**
30	**ENTREES**

30	**MUSHROOM MEDLEY**
32	**MELON AND PROSCIUTTO**
33	**STUFFED TOMATOES**
34	**GRILLED SCALLOPS WITH CURRIED TOMATO COULIS**
35	**SCALLOPS WITH BACON AND SPINACH**
36	**VEGETABLES**
36	**VEGETABLES IN MUSTARD VINAIGRETTE**
37	**POTATO AND CELERIAC PUREE**
37	**FRENCH BEANS**
38	**MAINS**
38	**VITELLO TONNATO**
40	**ROAST LEG OF LAMB WITH GARLIC-APRICOT GLAZE**
41	**BRAISED CHOPS WITH CAPSICUM**
42	**CHOOSING YOUR CHICKEN**
43	**CHICKEN AND BASIL**
44	**SPATCHCOCK**
46	**ROAST LEEKS WITH POTATOES AND BOCCONCINI**
48	**VEAL, EGGPLANT AND MOZZARELLA WITH PARSLEY PESTO**
50	**LAMB SKEWERS WITH COUSCOUS AND MINTED YOGHURT**
52	**DESSERTS**
52	**LEMON FEATHER CAKE**
54	**STRAWBERRY CUSTARDS**
55	**BAKED APPLES**
56	**FRUIT TARTS**
57	**GRILLED PEACHES WITH HONEY AND YOGHURT**
58	**PECAN PIE**
60	**TIPS**

THIS TRUCK IS DELIVERING CONVERSATION
TO A DINNER PARTY. SCRIPTS INCLUDE:

'WE WERE ABLE TO DO THE RENOVATIONS WHEN
CLINT STARTED DEFRAUDING THE BANK'

AND

'DID YOU KNOW THAT KEVIN IS A SERIAL KILLER?'

TONIGHT THE MOON IS FULL

Nelson Mandela has dropped by unexpectedly and goes pale when my first wife Imperia asks him to stay for dinner.

She has some wonderful qualities, Imperia, but cooking isn't one of them.

My old friend Chuck Berry is sitting at the baby grand and is playing 'How Long Can This Thing Last', He says he's not hungry.

We're giving a dinner party for eight. No-one's arrived and no-one's going to.

Nelson is leaning against Imperia's bookshelves with a triple scotch in his hand. His shaking hand.

The bookshelves Nelson is leaning against are where Imperia keeps her cookbooks. Eleven metres of them, measured across the spines.

Nelson says he has just remembered he has to go to the United Nations, and when he leaves Chuck Berry leaves with him.

A few minutes later Elliott Gould knocks on the glass panel beside the door.

I note his horrified face as he sees the dining table dressed to go. He disappears into the night.

No-one's arrived and no-one's going to.

Imperia's dinner parties are legend.

Like the last night on the Titanic is legend.

Tonight the moon is full.

A CLOSE FRIEND HIDING IN A CAVE
TO AVOID EATING AT ONE OF
IMPERIA'S DINNER PARTIES

DRESS-UP COOKING
CAN AMUSE YOUR GUESTS

IN DRESS-UP COOKING, THIS HAT HAS
A DEGREE OF DIFFICULTY OF KEVIN BACON

TERMINOLOGY

DEGLAZE

TO MAKE A GRAVY OR SAUCE BY ADDING WINE, WATER OR STOCK TO COOKING JUICES IN THE PAN, STIRRING IN ANY SEDIMENT AT THE BOTTOM STIR IN WELL, AND REDUCE, THEN STRAIN.

STOCKS

THE INTRODUCTION OF COMMERCIAL STOCK CUBES HAS TAKEN AWAY THE NECESSITY FOR LONG AND ARDUOUS HOURS IN THE KITCHEN MAKING TRADITIONAL STOCKS. HOWEVER, FOR THE PURIST, THERE ARE SOME SHORT CUTS TO HOMEMADE STOCKS. THESE WILL COMPLEMENT OTHERWISE PLAIN PIECES OF FISH, MEAT OR POULTRY, AND PUT SOME BODY INTO YOUR SOUPS.

BROWN STOCK

USE MEAT BONES AND CARROTS, CELERY AND ONION, BROWNED IN OIL. ADD $^1/_4$ LITRE/$^1/_2$ PINT WATER OR COOKING JUICES. REDUCE TO JELLY-LIKE CONSISTENCY. USE THIS FOR GRAVIES, BROWN SAUCES, BRAISED DISHES, STEWS AND FOR DEGLAZING. TO GO A STEP FURTHER, ADD 3 LITRES/$5^1/_4$ PINTS OF WATER, BRING TO BOIL, REDUCE AND SIMMER FOR 5-6 HOURS. KEEP SKIMMING OFF FROTH AND FAT DURING COOKING. STRAIN.

VEGETABLE STOCK

FRY A SELECTION OF CARROTS, ONIONS, CELERY, LEEKS AND HERBS IN BUTTER. ADD WATER AND BOIL. ADD PINCH OF SALT. REDUCE.

WHITE STOCK

USE VEAL BONES AND KNUCKLES. PUT MEAT, BONES AND A CHICKEN CARCASS IN A PAN WITH 3 LITRES/$5\frac{1}{4}$ PINTS OF WATER. BOIL AND SKIM. ADD CELERY, ONION, LEEKS AND CARROTS, ROUGHLY CHOPPED. ADD BOUQUET GARNI, SALT AND PEPPER. BOIL AND SIMMER FOR 3 HOURS, SKIMMING SEVERAL TIMES. STRAIN. USE TO MAKE WHITE SAUCES, WITH POACHED CHICKEN DISHES AND WITH PIECES OF FISH.

SAUCES

IN MANY LARGE COMMERCIAL KITCHENS, THE SAUCE CHEF IS A SPECIALIST, ALMOST REVERED. SAUCES ARE AN IMPORTANT PART OF YOUR END PRODUCT. EXAMPLES: VINAIGRETTE; MAYONNAISE; BROWN SAUCE; WHITE SAUCE; CURRY SAUCE; MEAT SAUCE; VEGETABLE SAUCE; CHEESE SAUCE; CREAM SAUCE; WINE SAUCE AND FRUIT SAUCE.

BASIC WHITE SAUCE

60g/$\frac{1}{4}$ CUP BUTTER

**60g/$\frac{1}{2}$ CUP FLOUR – THE BLEND
OF THESE TWO INGREDIENTS
IS CALLED A ROUX**

1 LITRE/1$\frac{3}{4}$ PINTS CHICKEN STOCK

MELT BUTTER. STIR IN FLOUR BRISKLY. GRADUALLY ADD STOCK. BRING TO BOIL, REDUCE HEAT AND COOK UNTIL DESIRED THICKNESS.

BECHAMEL SAUCE

MAKE THE ROUX AS FOR THE BASIC WHITE SAUCE, ADD MILK INSTEAD OF STOCK. USED FOR VEGETABLE, SOME FISH AND EGG DISHES.

TIP: MIXTURE MUST BE STIRRED CONSTANTLY WHEN ADDING MILK.

IN DRESS-UP COOKING,
THIS OUTFIT SCORES VERY POORLY

DRESSINGS

VINAIGRETTE

OLIVE OIL
VINEGAR
SALT AND PEPPER

DISSOLVE SALT IN VINEGAR. MIX 3 PARTS OIL TO 1 PART VINEGAR. ADD PEPPER. VINEGAR CAN BE REPLACED BY LEMON JUICE (IN THIS CASE $1/2$ OIL TO $1/2$ JUICE). OTHER INGREDIENTS MAY BE ADDED – MUSTARD, ESCHALOTS, GARLIC, CAPERS, HERBS, ONION, ETC. MIXTURE CAN BE PUT IN SCREW-TOP JAR AND SHAKEN.

MAYONNAISE

EGGS
OIL
VINEGAR OR LEMON JUICE
SALT AND PEPPER

PLACE 1-2 EGGS IN BLENDER. TURN ON LOW, GRADUALLY ADD OIL, A LITTLE AT A TIME. WHEN REQUIRED QUANTITY IS REACHED, START ADDING VINEGAR OR JUICE TO TASTE. KEEP BLENDING, AND MAYONNAISE WILL TURN INTO A WHITE, CREAMY CONSISTENCY. STIR IN SALT AND PEPPER. ALTERNATIVE ADDITION: 1-2 TEASPOONS MUSTARD ADDED TO EGGS.

GREEN MAYONNAISE

ADD 2 TABLESPOONS OF FINELY CHOPPED BASIL OR
PARSLEY OR WATERCRESS TO THE MAYONNAISE. MIX IN
VERY WELL.

AIOLI

AS FOR MAYONNAISE, BUT PUT A TORN PIECE OF
WHITE BREAD IN BLENDER FIRST WITH 2-3 CLOVES OF
GARLIC. GIVE IT A QUICK GO IN THE BLENDER. ADD
EGGS AND OTHER INGREDIENTS AS SPECIFIED. BREAD
CAN BE USED FOR NORMAL MAYONNAISE TOO, IT
TENDS TO PREVENT POSSIBILITY OF CURDLING.

IN DRESS-UP COOKING,
THIS OUTFIT HAS A DEGREE OF
DIFFICULTY OF .45 CALIBRE

HORS D'OEUVRES

STUFFED CHERRY TOMATOES

PUNNET OF CHERRY TOMATOES

125ml/$^1/_2$ CUP SOUR CREAM

**SALMON CAVIAR (RED OR BLACK
   CAN ALSO BE USED)**

FRESH DILL

HOLLOW TOMATOES, FILL WITH SOUR CREAM, TOP
WITH CAVIAR AND GARNISH WITH A SPRIG OF DILL.

IN DRESS-UP COOKING,
I THINK YOU'LL AGREE THAT THIS
THEME IS NOW WORN OUT

STEAK TARTARE

SERVES 4.

**1kg/2lb TOP-QUALITY MINCE – SIRLOIN
OR FILLET**
4 CLOVES GARLIC, FINELY CHOPPED
3 TEASPOONS CHOPPED CAPERS
3 DROPS OF TABASCO
60g/$\frac{1}{4}$ CUP OF WORCESTERSHIRE SAUCE
GROUND BLACK PEPPER AND SALT
3 SHALLOTS, FINELY CHOPPED
2 TABLESPOONS CHOPPED PARSLEY
3 BEATEN EGGS
2 TABLESPOONS OF DIJON MUSTARD

COMBINE ALL INGREDIENTS EXCEPT SHALLOTS AND
TASTE FOR CORRECT SEASONING, THEN MOULD INTO
ROUND SHAPE (SIMILAR TO LARGE BURGER PATTY).
YOU CAN PUT ONE WHOLE
EGG YOLK IN HOLE IN THE CENTRE OF EACH.

SERVE WITH TOAST CROUTONS.
GARNISH WITH SHALLOTS.

ELVIS MICHALOPOULOS, A MAN WHO IS A
POOR COOK, DEFLECTS ATTENTION FROM HIS
FOOD BY PUSHING A FAKE BEAR ON WHEELS
INTO THE DINING ROOM

SOUPS

ZUCCHINI AND CORIANDER SOUP

SERVES 4.

1 SPANISH ONION, CHOPPED

2 TABLESPOONS UNSALTED BUTTER

2kg/4lb ZUCCHINIS/COURGETTES, CUT INTO 1cm PIECES

SALT AND PEPPER

1 LITRE/1^3/$_4$ PINTS CHICKEN BROTH

2 LARGE HANDFULS OF CORIANDER

1 TABLESPOON FRESH LEMON JUICE

SOFTEN ONION IN BUTTER ON LOW HEAT.

ADD ZUCCHINI, SALT AND PEPPER AND COOK, COVERED, STIRRING OCCASIONALLY, FOR 5 MINUTES.

ADD BROTH AND SIMMER UNTIL ZUCCHINI IS TENDER – ABOUT 5 MINUTES.

REMOVE FROM HEAT, ADD CORIANDER AND LET COOL.

BLEND, STIRRING IN LEMON JUICE. CHECK SEASONING. SERVE AT ROOM TEMPERATURE OR CHILLED.

TOMATO AND TARRAGON SOUP

1 SPANISH ONION, SLICED

1 BAY LEAF

1kg/2lb RIPE TOMATOES

1 LITRE/$1^3/_4$ PINTS CHICKEN STOCK

OLIVE OIL

SALT AND PEPPER

1 CLOVE GARLIC, MINCED

12 FRESH TARRAGON LEAVES

$^1/_2$ TEASPOON SALT

1 TEASPOON CORNFLOUR MIXED WITH
   A LITTLE WATER

300ml/$^1/_2$ PINT TOMATO JUICE

1 TEASPOON WHITE SUGAR

HEAT OIL, ADD ONION AND FRY UNTIL TRANSLUCENT.

ADD TOMATOES, GARLIC AND SALT.

COVER AND SIMMER FOR ABOUT 45 MINUTES.

ADD OTHER INGREDIENTS EXCEPT TARRAGON LEAVES
AND CORNFLOUR/WATER MIX.

SIMMER FOR 30 MINUTES.

BLEND AND THEN BRING BACK TO BOIL. ADD
CORNFLOUR AND STIR FOR 5 MINUTES.

TAKE OFF AND THEN ADD TARRAGON.

CREAM OF JERUSALEM ARTICHOKE SOUP

1kg/2lb JERUSALEM ARTICHOKES
500ml/$^3/_4$ PINT MILK
1 TABLESPOON LEMON JUICE
3 TABLESPOONS CORNFLOUR
1 ONION, FINELY SLICED
6 TABLESPOONS COLD MILK
50g/2oz BUTTER
150ml/$^1/_4$ PINT WHIPPED CREAM
1 LITRE/1$^3/_4$ PINTS CHICKEN STOCK

GARNISH:

SALT AND PEPPER
12 HAZELNUTS, GRILLED
PINCH OF SUGAR
ROCK SALT

PEEL ARTICHOKES AND HOLD IN COLD WATER WITH DASH OF LEMON.

SWEAT ONION IN $^1/_2$ THE BUTTER UNTIL GOLDEN.

DRY AND SLICE ARTICHOKES, ADD TO FRYPAN.

ADD REST OF BUTTER AND LEMON JUICE, COVER ON LOW HEAT FOR 10 MINUTES, STIRRING OCCASIONALLY.

POUR IN STOCK, ADD SALT, PEPPER AND SUGAR.

SIMMER A FURTHER 20 MINUTES. BLEND.

RETURN PUREE TO POT AND STIR IN MILK,
USING A WHISK.

MIX CORNFLOUR WITH COLD MILK, ADD TO SOUP
AND BRING TO BOIL, STIRRING CONSTANTLY. GRIND
HAZELNUTS AND ROCK SALT. PLACE SOUP IN BOWLS
AND ADD A DOLLOP OF CREAM AND THE HAZELNUTS
BEFORE SERVING.

DINNER AT THE VAN GOGHS'

FRENCH ONION SOUP

1kg/2lb BROWN ONIONS
1$^3/_4$ LITRES/7 CUPS BOILING BEEF STOCK
112g/$^1/_2$ CUP BUTTER
250ml/1 CUP DRY WHITE WINE
1 FRENCH STICK (BAGUETTE),
 SLICED 2$^1/_2$cm THICK
1 TEASPOON SUGAR
1 TEASPOON SALT
200g/2 CUPS GRATED CHEESE – MIX OF
 CHEDDAR AND PARMESAN
4 TABLESPOONS FLOUR
250ml/1 CUP PORT

PUT BUTTER IN LARGE FRYPAN, ADD ONIONS AND
SIMMER GENTLY FOR 45 MINUTES, STIRRING
FREQUENTLY.

ADD SUGAR AND SALT AFTER THE FIRST 15 MINUTES.
ONIONS MUST BE DEEP GOLDEN BROWN.

ADD FLOUR AND STIR, COOKING A FURTHER 10
MINUTES.

ADD WINE AND REDUCE.

ADD STOCK AND SIMMER, SKIMMING, IF NECESSARY,
FOR 45 MINUTES.

ADD PORT BEFORE SERVING.

SERVE IN LARGE BOWLS, WITH TOASTED BAGUETTE
ROUNDS, GRATED CHEESE AND PLENTY OF CRACKED
PEPPER (MELT CHEESE ONTO BAGUETTES FIRST).

VICHYSSOISE

12 MEDIUM POTATOES, PEELED

8 LARGE LEEKS (WHITE PART ONLY), SLICED

4 TABLESPOONS BUTTER

1 TABLESPOON SALT

1 1/4 LITRES/5 CUPS CHICKEN BROTH

250ml/1 CUP MILK

250ml/1 CUP CREAM

PINCH OF NUTMEG

WHITE PEPPER

250ml/1 CUP HEAVY CREAM

CHIVES FOR GARNISH

HEAT BUTTER AND SAUTE LEEKS 15 MINUTES.

ADD POTATOES, SALT AND CHICKEN BROTH AND COOK UNTIL POTATOES ARE SOFT, ABOUT 30 MINUTES.

PUREE MIXTURE, MAKING SURE THERE ARE NO LUMPS.

ADD THE MILK AND CREAM, NUTMEG AND PEPPER.

SERVE HOT OR CHILLED.

IS GREAT AS A SUMMER SOUP.

BEFORE SERVING, STIR IN CREAM AND GARNISH WITH CHOPPED CHIVES.

MUSHROOM VICHYSSOISE

6 LEEKS (WHITE ONLY), WASHED WELL

6 POTATOES, PEELED

3 TABLESPOONS BUTTER

**1kg/2lb MUSHROOMS (WILD OR DRIED),
   SOAKED UNTIL SOFT**

SALT

1 LITRE/$1^3/_4$ PINTS RICH CHICKEN STOCK

125ml/$^1/_2$ CUP MILK

125ml/$^1/_2$ CUP CREAM

SALT, PEPPER, NUTMEG

125ml/$^1/_2$ CUP HEAVY CREAM

PARSLEY FOR GARNISH

SAUTE LEEKS IN THE BUTTER ON LOW HEAT UNTIL SOFT.

DO NOT BROWN.

ADD POTATOES, MUSHROOMS, SALT AND STOCK.

SIMMER ABOUT 30 MINUTES UNTIL POTATOES
ARE TENDER.

PUREE.

ADD THE MILK AND CREAM MIX AND SEASON WITH
SALT, PEPPER AND NUTMEG. CHILL.

BEFORE SERVING, STIR IN CREAM AND GARNISH
WITH CHOPPED PARSLEY.

PRAWN, MUD CRAB AND MANGO

1 MUD CRAB

$^1/_2$kg/1lb COOKED PRAWNS

1 LARGE MANGO

1 LARGE AVOCADO

MIXTURE OF LEAVES – ROCKET, WATERCRESS, COS, LAMB LETTUCE, CORIANDER

DRESSING:

125ml/$^1/_2$ CUP FRESHLY SQUEEZED ORANGE JUICE

125ml/$^1/_2$ CUP SESAME OIL

60ml/$^1/_4$ CUP LIME JUICE

2 TEASPOONS GRAIN MUSTARD

2 TEASPOONS SUGAR

SALT AND PEPPER

CRACK AND SHELL MUD CRAB. ARRANGE LEAVES ON INDIVIDUAL PLATES AND PUT CRABMEAT IN CENTRE. ARRANGE AVOCADO, MANGO AND PRAWNS IN FAN SHAPE AROUND EDGE OF PLATE. MIX DRESSING INGREDIENTS TOGETHER AND SPOON OVER TOP.

ENTREES

MUSHROOM MEDLEY

6 LARGE MUSHROOMS

6 LARGE BUTTON MUSHROOMS

15 OYSTER MUSHROOMS

12 SHITAKE MUSHROOMS

1 BAGUETTE, CUT INTO ROUNDS, ALLOW 3 PIECES PER PERSON

3 TABLESPOONS BUTTER

1/3 BUNCH SHALLOTS, FINELY SLICED

3 TABLESPOONS FINELY CHOPPED CORIANDER

SALT AND PEPPER

375ml/1 1/2 CUPS CREAM

TOAST BAGUETTE ROUNDS.

SOAK LARGE MUSHROOMS 20-30 MINUTES.

MELT BUTTER IN PAN.

STIR IN BUTTON MUSHROOMS, SHALLOTS, CORIANDER, SALT AND PEPPER.

STIR IN CREAM AND THICKEN, WITHOUT BOILING.

COOK UNTIL SOFT.

BRUSH OYSTER AND LARGE MUSHROOMS WITH BUTTER
AND GRILL ON BOTH SIDES. ON INDIVIDUAL PLATES,
PUT LARGE MUSHROOM IN CENTRE ON ONE OF
BAGUETTE ROUNDS.

HEAP BUTTON MUSHROOMS ON TOP.

ADD ANOTHER TOAST ROUND, THEN PLACE OYSTER
AND SHITAKE MUSHROOMS ON THE TOP.

POUR CREAM SAUCE OVER THE PYRAMID.

APPARENTLY, JOHN MAJOR GIVES WELDING
DEMONSTRATIONS AT HIS DINNER PARTIES IF THE
CONVERSATION FLAGS, AS IT INEVITABLY DOES

MELON AND PROSCIUTTO

1 HONEYDEW MELON

1 ROCKMELON

¹/₂ kg/1 lb PROSCIUTTO, THINLY SLICED

1 LEMON OR LIME

SEED AND PEEL MELONS, CUT INTO THIN SLICES.

ALLOW 2-3 SLICES OF BOTH MELONS PER PERSON.

WRAP EACH PIECE WITH 2-3 SLICES OF PROSCIUTTO
AND ARRANGE ON INDIVIDUAL PLATES.

GARNISH WITH A WEDGE OF LEMON OR LIME.

VARIATION: YOU CAN SUBSTITUTE MANGO,
PAWPAW
OR FRESH FIGS FOR MELON.

PARCELS AT THE DINNER TABLE CAN
SOMETIMES AMUSE THE GUESTS MORE
THAN DRESS-UP COOKING

STUFFED TOMATOES

6 FIRM TOMATOES
3 200g/7oz CANS TUNA (DRAINED)
CHIVES, CHOPPED
150ml/$^1/_2$ CUP LEMON MAYONNAISE
350g/12oz MUSHROOMS, CHOPPED
25g/$^3/_4$ oz BUTTER
SALT AND PEPPER
$^1/_2$ BUNCH OF BASIL
WATERCRESS FOR GARNISH

USE HOMEMADE MAYONNAISE WITH LEMON JUICE (SEE PAGE 12). SAUTE CHOPPED MUSHROOMS IN THE BUTTER UNTIL SOFT AND ALMOST PUREED.

ADD SALT AND PEPPER. CUT TOMATOES IN HALF AND SCOOP OUT FLESH. PUT TUNA IN WITH BASIL, MUSHROOM PUREE AND ADD MAYONNAISE. SPOON MIXTURE INTO TOMATOES AND SPRINKLE WITH CHIVES. TO SERVE, GARNISH PLATE WITH WATERCRESS.

SOME HAVE DISCOVERED THAT OPENING A
PARCEL THAT HAS MARLON BRANDO IN IT,
IF ANYTHING, REDUCES CONVERSATION

GRILLED SCALLOPS WITH CURRIED TOMATO COULIS

4 SHALLOTS

3 TABLESPOONS OLIVE OIL

2 TEASPOONS MUSTARD SEEDS

2 TEASPOONS GOOD QUALITY CURRY POWDER

1 TEASPOON SUGAR

8 PLUM TOMATOES, CHOPPED

SALT AND PEPPER

3 TEASPOONS BALSAMIC VINEGAR

750g/1$\frac{1}{2}$lb SCALLOPS

COOK SHALLOTS IN OLIVE OIL UNTIL SOFT.

ADD MUSTARD SEEDS AND CURRY POWDER. COOK, STIRRING, FOR 1 MINUTE. STIR IN SUGAR, TOMATOES, SALT AND PEPPER AND COOK FOR 3 MINUTES, OR UNTIL TOMATOES BEGIN TO RELEASE THEIR JUICE.

STIR IN BALSAMIC VINEGAR AND KEEP WARM.

HEAT A GRILL PAN. BRUSH WITH OIL.

ADD SCALLOPS AND GRILL FOR 2$\frac{1}{2}$ MINUTES ON EACH SIDE, OR UNTIL JUST FIRM. PLACE COULIS ON PLATES AND HEAP SCALLOPS ON TOP.

GARNISH WITH A SPRIG OF GREENERY.

SCALLOPS WITH BACON AND SPINACH

SERVES 4.

16 LARGE TASMANIAN SEA SCALLOPS
2 RASHERS STREAKY BACON
4 HANDFULS OF BABY SPINACH
SALT AND PEPPER
WHITE WINE VINEGAR
4 TABLESPOONS OLIVE OIL

REMOVE SCALLOPS FROM REFRIGERATOR TO BRING TO ROOM TEMPERATURE.

SEASON SPINACH WITH SALT AND PEPPER.

TOSS SPINACH WITH OLIVE OIL.

ARRANGE SPINACH ON 4 SERVING PLATES.

DRIZZLE WHITE WINE VINEGAR OVER SPINACH LEAVES. CUT BACON INTO CUBES AND SAUTE IN A NON-STICK FRYING PAN UNTIL CRISPY.

DRAIN OFF EXCESS FAT, SPREAD OVER SPINACH.

HEAT FRYING PAN UNTIL ALMOST SMOKING.

ADD THE SCALLOPS, ALLOW 30 SECONDS EACH SIDE.

PLACE ON SPINACH LEAVES. SERVE.

VEGETABLES

VEGETABLES IN MUSTARD VINAIGRETTE

CAULIFLOWER, CUT INTO FLOWERETS

BROCCOLI, CUT INTO FLOWERETS

FRESH ASPARAGUS

GREEN BEANS

SNOW PEAS

CARROTS, CHOPPED INTO SMALL CHUNKS

6 SHALLOTS, FINELY CHOPPED

PARSLEY, TARRAGON, DILL

VINAIGRETTE:

250ml/1 CUP TARRAGON VINEGAR

1 TABLESPOON DIJON MUSTARD

250ml/1 CUP OLIVE OIL

SALT AND GROUND PEPPER

BLANCH AND REFRESH VEGETABLES.

WHISK VINAIGRETTE INGREDIENTS TOGETHER AND POUR OVER VEGETABLES.

POTATO AND CELERIAC PUREE

400g/14oz CELERIAC
350g/12oz POTATOES
25g/$^3/_4$ oz BUTTER
SALT AND PEPPER
HOT MILK

PEEL THE VEGETABLES AND CUT INTO PIECES.

BOIL IN SALTED WATER UNTIL TENDER.

DRAIN AND ALLOW TO STEAM DRY.

MASH WITH BUTTER AND SALT AND PEPPER.

ADD HOT MILK AND BEAT UNTIL LIGHT AND FLUFFY.

FRENCH BEANS

500g/1lb FRENCH BEANS
15g/$^1/_2$ oz BUTTER
BLACK GROUND PEPPER
SALT
FRESH GRATED PARMESAN

TOP AND TAIL BEANS AND PUT INTO RAPIDLY
BOILING WATER FOR A COUPLE OF MINUTES.

REMOVE AND IMMEDIATELY REFRESH.

THIS CAN BE DONE AHEAD OF TIME.

WHEN READY TO SERVE THE MEAL, QUICKLY FRY
BEANS IN BUTTER, REMOVE TO SERVING DISH, ADD
SALT AND PEPPER.

SPRINKLE WITH PARMESAN.

MAINS

VITELLO TONNATO

1.25kg/3lb BONED LEG VEAL
1 185g/7oz CAN TUNA, DRAINED
5 ANCHOVY FILLETS, FINELY CHOPPED
1 ONION, FINELY CHOPPED
250ml/1 CUP WHITE WINE
125ml/$^1/_2$ CUP WATER
125ml/$^1/_2$ CUP WHITE VINEGAR
SALT AND PEPPER
$^1/_2$ BUNCH BASIL
DRY OREGANO
OLIVE OIL
2 HARD-BOILED EGG YOLKS, MASHED
CAPERS, FINELY CHOPPED
LEMON SLICES FOR GARNISH
CHOPPED PARSLEY

PUT ALL INGREDIENTS UP TO OLIVE OIL IN A LARGE PAN AND BRING TO BOIL.

REDUCE HEAT, COVER AND SIMMER GENTLY FOR 1 $^1/_2$ HOURS OR UNTIL MEAT IS TENDER.

PLACE VEAL ASIDE AND BEAT OLIVE OIL INTO SAUCE UNTIL SMOOTH AND SLIGHTLY RUNNY.

BEAT IN EGG YOLKS UNTIL SMOOTH.

ADD CHOPPED CAPERS.

CUT VEAL INTO SLICES AND PLACE ON SERVING PLATTER. SPREAD WITH SAUCE AND PLACE IN REFRIGERATOR OVERNIGHT.

GARNISH WITH LEMON AND SPRINKLE WITH PARSLEY.

SERVE WITH CRISP GREEN SALAD AND ITALIAN PICKLES.

SYMPHONY ORCHESTRAS IN YOUR DINING ROOM CAN BE A HELPFUL DIVERSION IF THE LEG VEAL IS A BIT OVERCOOKED

ROAST LEG OF LAMB WITH GARLIC-APRICOT GLAZE

500ml/2 CUPS WHITE WINE

1 LEG OF LAMB, RUBBED WITH SALT AND PEPPER

3 CLOVES GARLIC, CUT INTO SLIVERS

FRESH ROSEMARY SPRIGS

1 SMALL JAR APRICOT JAM

PIERCE LAMB IN SEVERAL PLACES WITH THE POINT OF A SHARP KNIFE, STUFF WITH GARLIC SLIVERS AND ROSEMARY. POUR WINE OVER THE TOP.

SPREAD ON SOME OF THE JAM AND BAKE AT 180°C/350°F/GAS MARK 4 FOR ABOUT $1\frac{1}{2}$ HOURS, BASTING OCCASIONALLY WITH THE REST OF THE JAM.

LET THE LAMB STAND FOR ABOUT 15 MINUTES BEFORE SERVING.

BRAISED CHOPS WITH CAPSICUMS

60g/½ CUP FLOUR

1 LARGE CHOP PER PERSON – LAMB, VEAL OR PORK

2 TEASPOONS VEGETABLE OIL

250ml/1 CUP CHICKEN BROTH

5 TEASPOONS BALSAMIC VINEGAR

150g/1½ CUPS EACH OF CHOPPED GREEN, RED AND YELLOW CAPSICUM

2 TEASPOONS CORNFLOUR DISSOLVED IN 4 TEASPOONS WATER

IN NON–STICK FRYPAN, HEAT OIL OVER MODERATELY HIGH HEAT. DUST CHOPS IN FLOUR AND THEN PUT IN PAN.

BROWN THE CHOPS, SEASON WITH SALT AND PEPPER.

ADD BROTH AND VINEGAR, BRINGING LIQUID TO THE BOIL.

TRANSFER MIXTURE TO A BAKING DISH LARGE ENOUGH TO HAVE CHOPS IN ONE LAYER.

SPRINKLE WITH CAPSICUMS AND PUT IN THE OVEN, COVERED WITH FOIL, ON MEDIUM FOR 15 MINUTES.

STIR CORNFLOUR MIX INTO COOKING JUICES AND PUT ON STOVE FOR 5 MINUTES.

SERVE WITH PASTA AND GREEN SALAD.

CHOOSING YOUR CHICKEN

IF YOU ARE LOOKING FOR A ROASTING CHICKEN, CHOOSE A FATTY, PLUMP ONE, AS THE FAT STOPS THE CHICKEN FROM DRYING OUT DURING COOKING.

FOR ROASTING, SPRINKLE WITH THYME, TARRAGON OR ROSEMARY AND LEMON JUICE.

TO CHECK IF IT IS READY, STICK A SKEWER IN AND IF THE FLUID RUNNING OUT IS CLEAR (NO BLOOD), THE CHOOK IS READY.

FOR A CHICKEN CASSEROLE, CHOOSE A PLUMP BIRD BUT NOT FATTY, AS THE FAT JUST SETTLES IN AND ON YOUR SAUCE. IN A CASSEROLE, ADD ONIONS, CARROTS, FENNEL, MUSHROOMS, GARLIC, PEPPERS AND HERBS (ALL OR ANY OF THESE).

FOR POACHING, CHOOSE A LARGE, PLUMP BIRD, BUT NOT TOO FATTY.

PARCELS OF PYTHONS SHOULD BE
CAREFULLY WRAPPED, BUT ARE NOT
AS POPULAR AS YOU THINK

CHICKEN AND BASIL

SAUTE A QUARTERED CHICKEN DUSTED IN FLOUR IN A MIXTURE OF OIL AND BUTTER UNTIL BROWN.

DRAIN ON ABSORBENT PAPER.

ARRANGE ON SERVING PLATTER.

ADD 180ml/ $3/4$ CUP OF WHITE WINE TO THE COOKING PAN AND DEGLAZE.

WHISK IN 4 TABLESPOONS COLD BUTTER, CUT IN PIECES.

ADD 1-2 TABLESPOONS CHOPPED BASIL. STIR IN WELL AND POUR OVER CHICKEN.

KEVIN BACON HAS FOUND A WAY TO LEAVE DINNER PARTIES IF THEY ARE NOT ENTERTAINING. HE KEEPS A REMOTE CONTROL IN HIS POCKET AND WHEN HE PRESSES IT, A TRAPDOOR OPENS IN THE ROOF OF HIS CAR AND FLASHING LIGHTS AND A PUBLIC ADDRESS SYSTEM ENGAGE. THE P.A. BOOMS OUT, 'THE LOCAL HYDRO-ELECTRIC DAM HAS BROKEN AND THERE IS A 10 METRE WALL OF WATER HEADING TOWARDS THIS ADDRESS. YOU HAVE 3 MINUTES TO DRIVE TO HIGH GROUND.' KEVIN BEATS EVERYONE TO THE DOOR

SPATCHCOCK

1 SPATCHCOCK PER PERSON

CUT AN APPLE IN QUARTERS, POKE 2 CLOVES IN EACH PIECE AND PUT INSIDE EACH BIRD, WITH 1 BAY LEAF. POUR 1 NIP OF BRANDY INTO EACH BIRD. CLOSE BIRD WITH TOOTHPICK

1 ONION, CUT IN QUARTERS

1 CARROT, ROUGHLY DICED

3 STICKS CELERY

4 CLOVES

6 SPRIGS PARSLEY

2 BAY LEAVES

SALT AND PEPPER

WATER

DRY WHITE WINE

2 TABLESPOONS BUTTER

MAKE A VEGETABLE STOCK IN THE BASE
OF A BAKING DISH:
ADD ONION, CARROT, CELERY, 4 CLOVES, 6 SPRIGS
PARSLEY, 2 BAY LEAVES, SALT AND PEPPER.

USE HALF-WATER, HALF-WINE TO COVER VEGETABLES.

SIT SPATCHCOCKS SIDE BY SIDE, COVER WITH FOIL
AND PLACE IN A PREHEATED MODERATE OVEN.

COOK FOR 30 MINUTES, REMOVE FOIL, COOK A FINAL 10-15 MINUTES ON HIGH TO BROWN.

REMOVE SPATCHCOCKS TO A WARMED SERVING PLATTER.

STRAIN STOCK, ADD CHOPPED BUTTER, WHISK.

ADD SALT AND PEPPER AND CHOPPED PARSLEY.

POUR SAUCE OVER BIRDS.

SERVE WITH GREEN SALAD AND CRUSTY BREAD TO SOAK UP THE SAUCE.

ROAST LEEKS WITH POTATOES AND BOCCONCINI

SERVES 4.

8 BABY LEEKS

500g/1lb BABY NEW POTATOES

1 TEASPOON FRESH THYME LEAVES

4 TABLESPOONS OLIVE OIL

2 FRESH BOCCONCINI (BABY MOZZARELLA)

2 CLOVES GARLIC

1 BIRDS EYE CHILLI, SPLIT AND SEEDED

4 PARSLEY SPRIGS

1 HANDFUL ROCKET SALAD LEAVES

CUT BOCCONCINI INTO 1cm THICK SLICES.

PLACE IN BOWL WITH OLIVE OIL TO COVER, GARLIC, CHILLI AND PARSLEY SPRIGS. COVER AND REFRIGERATE OVERNIGHT.

BOIL POTATOES UNTIL JUST COOKED, REFRESH UNDER COLD WATER.

CUT INTO BITE-SIZE PIECES.

PREHEAT OVEN TO 180°C/350°F/GAS MARK 4.

TRIM LEEKS, BLANCH IN BOILING WATER 3 MINUTES. REFRESH UNDER COLD WATER, DRAIN AND PAT DRY WITH PAPER TOWEL.

HEAT 2 TABLESPOONS OF OLIVE OIL IN A BAKING DISH

ON STOVE OVER MEDIUM HEAT. ADD LEEKS
AND TOSS GENTLY.

PLACE IN OVEN FOR 12 MINUTES.

REMOVE FROM OVEN. SET OVEN TO
HIGH TEMPERATURE.

PLACE BAKING TRAY OVER MEDIUM HEAT
ON STOVE TOP.

ADD REMAINING OLIVE OIL. ADD POTATOES, TOSS
AND SEASON.

PLACE IN OVEN, ROAST UNTIL GOLDEN, ADD THYME
LEAVES 5 MINUTES BEFORE END OF COOKING.

ARRANGE POTATOES AND LEEKS ON SERVING PLATES.

TOP WITH ROCKET LETTUCE AND BOCCONCINI.

SPRINKLE WITH CHOPPED PARSLEY. SERVE.

VEAL, EGGPLANT AND MOZZARELLA WITH PARSLEY PESTO

SERVES 4.

4 VEAL SCALOPPINE (CUT IN HALF)
2 MEDIUM EGGPLANTS/AUBERGINES
SALT AND PEPPER
3 HANDFULS OF PARSLEY SPRIGS
1 CLOVE OF GARLIC, CRUSHED
2 TABLESPOONS PARMESAN CHEESE, GRATED
3 TABLESPOONS OLIVE OIL
4 MOZZARELLA CHEESE SLICES

FRY THE VEAL IN OLIVE OIL UNTIL GOLDEN, CUT EGGPLANT INTO 2CM THICK SLICES, SPRINKLE WITH SALT, LEAVE FOR 30 MINUTES.

DRAIN WELL AND DRY WITH PAPER TOWEL.

BRUSH EGGPLANT WITH OLIVE OIL AND GRILL UNTIL GOLDEN BROWN.

PREHEAT OVEN TO 220°C/425°F/GAS MARK 7.

ON A BAKING SHEET, LAYER EGGPLANT, VEAL, EGGPLANT, VEAL. TOP WITH MOZZARELLA CHEESE.

BAKE IN OVEN UNTIL CHEESE BEGINS TO MELT (ABOUT 10 MINUTES).

SERVE WITH PARSLEY PESTO DRIZZLED OVER AND AROUND.

PARSLEY PESTO:

PUT PARSLEY IN BLENDER WITH PARMESAN CHEESE AND GARLIC.

WITH BLENDER OPERATING, SLOWLY ADD 6 TABLESPOONS OF OLIVE OIL.

LAMB SKEWERS WITH COUSCOUS AND MINTED YOGHURT

500g/1lb LAMB LEG, CUBED

1 RED CAPSICUM

1 GREEN CAPSICUM

1 LARGE SPANISH ONION

2 MEDIUM ZUCCHINIS

6 BUTTON MUSHROOMS

1 BUNCH PARSLEY

1 BUNCH THYME

250ml/1 CUP OLIVE OIL

2 CLOVES OF GARLIC, CHOPPED

SALT AND PEPPER

1 PACKET COUSCOUS

JUICE OF 1 LEMON

2 TEASPOONS OF CHOPPED MINT

CUT ONION AND CAPSICUM INTO $2^1/_2$ cm SQUARES.

THREAD MEAT, ONION AND CAPSICUM ON SKEWERS IN ALTERNATE PATTERN.

CHOP PARSLEY, THYME AND GARLIC.

MIX WITH OLIVE OIL.

ADD SALT AND PEPPER.

POUR OVER SKEWERS AND MARINATE FOR 4 HOURS
OR OVERNIGHT.

MAKE COUSCOUS ACCORDING TO INSTRUCTIONS.
FINELY DICE LEFTOVER CAPSICUMS, ONION,
MUSHROOMS, ZUCCHINIS.

ADD TO COUSCOUS WITH LEMON JUICE. MIX WELL.
DRAIN OIL FROM MARINADE.

GRILL SKEWERS UNTIL GOLDEN.

SERVE WITH COUSCOUS AND MINTED YOGHURT.

DESSERTS

LEMON FEATHER CAKE

6 EGGS
275g/10oz CASTOR SUGAR
1 LEMON
150g/5oz FLOUR
SIFTED ICING SUGAR

FILLING:

300ml/$^1/_2$ PINT DOUBLE CREAM
225g/8oz LEMON CURD

PREHEAT OVEN TO 180°C/350°F/GAS MARK 4.

BUTTER A CAKE OR SANDWICH TIN AND LINE
WITH GREASEPROOF PAPER.

DUST WITH ICING SUGAR AND FLOUR.

SEPARATE EGGS.

BEAT YOLKS AND SUGAR TOGETHER WITH JUICE AND
GRATED LEMON RIND, UNTIL LIGHT IN COLOUR AND
THICK IN TEXTURE.

ADD FLOUR AND BEAT THOROUGHLY.

WHISK EGG WHITES UNTIL THICK AND FORMING
PEAKS, FOLD INTO MIXTURE.

POUR INTO CAKE TIN AND BAKE IN PREHEATED OVEN FOR 50-60 MINUTES. COOL.

FOR THE FILLING, WHIP CREAM UNTIL FIRM AND ADD LEMON CURD. STIR WELL.

USING A SHARP, SERRATED KNIFE, SLIT THE CAKE IN TWO AND FILL WITH LEMON CREAM.

PUT TOP OF CAKE BACK ON AND DUST WITH ICING SUGAR.

A WELL-KNOWN SOPRANO PERFORMING
DURING DESSERT CAN LIFT THE FLAGGING
SPIRITS OF THE GUESTS

STRAWBERRY CUSTARDS

3 PUNNETS STRAWBERRIES

8 EGG YOLKS

8 TEASPOONS ICING SUGAR

200ml/$^1/_3$ PINT CREAM

1 TEASPOON CINNAMON

USE A 15cm SHALLOW OVEN DISH OR
MEDIUM-SIZED RAMEKIN PER PERSON.

HALVE STRAWBERRIES AND COVER BOTTOM OF
DISHES. WHISK YOLKS, SUGAR AND CREAM LIGHTLY,
POUR OVER BERRIES (IT WILL NOT COMPLETELY
COVER BERRIES).

SPRINKLE WITH CINNAMON.

BAKE IN MODERATE OVEN UNTIL SET – 15-20 MINUTES.
CAN BE SERVED HOT OR COLD.

SERVE WITH CREAM, ICE-CREAM, OR JUST ON
ITS OWN.

BAKED APPLES

6 LARGE GRANNY SMITH APPLES
A COUPLE OF KNOBS OF BUTTER
PER APPLE
HONEY
CINNAMON
BRANDY

PEEL AND CORE APPLES.

PLACE IN BAKING DISH WITH A LITTLE OF THE BUTTER,
HONEY, CINNAMON AND BRANDY POURED INTO
CENTRE OF EACH APPLE.

PUT SOME BUTTER AROUND BASE OF APPLES.

POUR HONEY OVER TOP OF APPLES AND SPRINKLE
WITH EXTRA CINNAMON.

COVER WITH FOIL AND BAKE IN MODERATE OVEN
FOR 1 HOUR.

DO NOT OVERCOOK; APPLES MUST KEEP THEIR SHAPE.

BASTE FREQUENTLY DURING COOKING.

SERVE WITH CARAMELISED LIQUID POURED OVER APPLES
AND WITH CREAM AND/OR ICE-CREAM.

FRUIT TARTS

FROZEN SHORTCRUST PASTRY

VANILLA PASTRY CREAM OR CREME ANGLAISE (CUSTARD)

STRAWBERRIES, KIWI FRUIT, RASPBERRIES, MANDARIN SEGMENTS (PIPS REMOVED)

ROLL OUT PASTRY AND LINE CUP-CAKE TINS (PATTY TINS).

PRICK BASE OF EACH WITH A FORK AND BAKE UNTIL BROWNED.

REMOVE FROM TINS IMMEDIATELY AND COOL.

PUT A DROP OF CUSTARD IN EACH TART BASE AND COVER COMPLETELY WITH FRUIT.

ALWAYS LOCK YOUR DOG OUTSIDE THE HOUSE. DOGS ARE UNRELIABLE AT DINNER PARTIES

GRILLED PEACHES WITH HONEY AND YOGHURT

SERVES 4.

4 PEACHES, FIRM BUT RIPE
4 TABLESPOONS HONEY
JUICE OF ONE LEMON
4 TEASPOONS BUTTER
200g/7oz PLAIN YOGHURT
4 MINT SPRIGS
28g/$^1/_4$ CUP PISTACHIO KERNELS

IN BOWL, MIX HONEY AND LEMON JUICE.

CUT PEACHES IN HALF AND REMOVE STONES.

LIE PEACHES ON A BAKING SHEET, CUT SIDE UP.

BRUSH WITH HONEY AND LEMON JUICE MIXTURE AND DAB BUTTER ON TOP.

PLACE UNDER PREHEATED HOT GRILL FOR 7 MINUTES.

CUT LARGE LEAVES FROM MINT SPRIGS, LEAVING SMALLER TIPS FOR GARNISH.

CHOP LARGE LEAVES OF MINT AND MIX WITH YOGHURT.

REMOVE PEACHES TO SERVING PLATES, SPOON IN YOGHURT, SCATTER WITH PISTACHIO KERNELS.

SERVE.

PECAN PIE

250g/9oz SHORTCRUST PASTRY SHEETS

150g/5oz GOLDEN SYRUP

100g/4oz BROWN SUGAR

3 EGGS

80g/3oz UNSALTED BUTTER

30g/1oz PLAIN FLOUR

$\frac{1}{2}$ TEASPOON VANILLA ESSENCE

4 TEASPOONS COCOA POWDER

**250g/1$\frac{1}{2}$ CUPS PECAN NUTS
(HALVES ARE BEST)**

**3 TABLESPOONS GRATED DARK
  CHOCOLATE**

PREHEAT OVEN TO 180°C/350°F/GAS MARK 4.

LINE 250mm WIDE PIE TIN WITH PASTRY.

PRICK PASTRY WITH FORK AND BAKE FOR 30 MINUTES
OR UNTIL GOLDEN BROWN.

BAKE PECAN HALVES IN OVEN FOR 5 MINUTES.

IN A SMALL POT, HEAT GOLDEN SYRUP AND SUGAR
AND MIX WELL.

REMOVE FROM HEAT. ALLOW TO COOL SLIGHTLY
AND ADD TO LIGHTLY BEATEN EGGS.

STIR IN MELTED BUTTER, FLOUR, VANILLA ESSENCE
AND COCOA.

SET OVEN TEMPERATURE TO 170°C/325°F/GAS MARK 3.

POUR SOME SYRUP MIXTURE INTO PASTRY CASE AND
SPREAD EVENLY AND GENTLY.

PLACE PECAN NUTS IN NEAT PATTERN OVER THE PIE.

POUR ON THE REMAINING SYRUP MIXTURE.

BAKE FOR 30 MINUTES OR UNTIL SET.

ALLOW TO COOL SLIGHTLY.

SERVE WITH WHIPPED CREAM AND GRATED
CHOCOLATE.

TIPS

IF YOU RUN OUT OF TIME, INSPIRATION, OR ARE JUST PLAIN LOUSY AT MAKING DESSERTS, NOTHING BEATS A SELECTION OF INTERESTING AND VARIED CHEESES ACCOMPANIED BY FRESH BERRIES, KIWI FRUIT CUT IN WEDGES AND APPLE WEDGES.

SERVE YUMMY CHOCOLATES AND PETIT FOURS WITH PLUNGER COFFEE.

IF DRESS-UP COOKING,
GENERAL WEIRDNESS AND
PARCELS AREN'T FOR YOU,
THEN THERE'S SET BUILDING.

YOU MOVE OUT THE FURNITURE
AND THEN, JUST LIKE THE
MOVIES, YOU BUILD A SET.

A DESERT

A BEACH

A CROCODILE POND